HE LEADS

Mountain Gorilla, the Gentle Giant

Published by Familius LLC, www. Familius.com
PO Box 1249 Reedley, CA 93654

Familius books are available at special discounts,
whether for bulk purchases for sales promotions, or for family or corporate use.
For more information, email orders@familius.com

Library of Congress Control Number:
2021946011

Print ISBN 9781641706483
Ebook ISBN 9781641706780
KF 9781641707145
FE 9781641706964

Printed in China
Edited by Lacey Wulf and Erin Lund
Book and cover design by Brooke Jorden
Illustrations by Yumi Shimokawara

109876543
First Edition

HE LEADS

Mountain Gorilla, the Gentle Giant

June Smalls

Illustrations by Yumi Shimokawara

He is the king.
He leads his family, his troop.

Mountain gorillas are apes, closely related to humans. They live in complex social groups known as troops or bands that range in size from two to thirty gorillas.

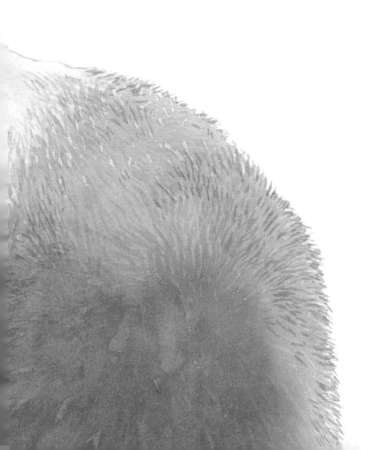

His silver back shows his age and experience.

The troop is led by a dominant male, usually the eldest in the group. His hair is black, but as he ages, it forms a silver saddle on his back. This is where the name "silverback" comes from. The largest of the great apes, male gorillas can be up to 6 feet tall and weigh more than 400 pounds. The smaller female can be up to 5 feet tall and weigh more 200 pounds.

Mountain gorillas live in the steep mountain forests of central Africa. They walk on all fours, using their knuckles to carry the weight of the front of their bodies. This is called knuckle-walking. They live in territories of about sixteen square miles, but only travel about half a mile each day.

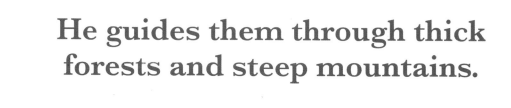

He guides them through thick forests and steep mountains.

It is up to him to find a safe area to forage for food.

These herbivores live on a diet of roots, shoots, fruit, wild celery, and tree bark and pulp. They rarely drink water, getting what they need from the vegetation they eat. They have powerful jaw muscles that help them chew tough vegetation. They will also eat insects and small animals. An adult gorilla can eat between 40 and 75 pounds of vegetation each day.

And where they stop for midday socializing.

The middle of the day is for resting, grooming, and playing. Social grooming is an integral part of the gorilla lifestyle as it helps them forge family bonds. The youngsters especially use this time to play, wrestle, and climb.

He has the power to throw ten times his weight, but he is mostly gentle and shy.

The adult male gorilla has the strength to flip a car, and his canines can grow up to 2 inches long. These large mammals are intimidating, but the gorilla is mostly a calm creature, content to lounge and eat most of the day. They are difficult to find in the thick mountain forests, and the dominant silverback will lead his troop away from any potential danger.

The young ones romp, and the mighty silverback curbs his strength to play with and groom them.

The adults will also play with the young. Wrestling gently, the adults control their strength so they do not harm the little ones. This play teaches the young social skills.

Gorillas communicate in many ways, including sounds like grunts or barks, touching, posturing, and even scent. Silverback males can give off a unique scent that can raise an alarm within the group without having to make any noise.

But if a member of his troop misbehaves, he will display his dominance.

Gorillas perform displays of aggression when they are threatened or need to keep their troop in order. This includes loud chest beats, the sound of which is amplified by air sacks extending into their chests, as well as growls, howls, barks, and roars. They may stand upright, throw things, or charge at their opponent. They can also hit and bite.

They travel again to find a place to nest for the night.

Each night, the gorilla troop will make new nests on the ground. Each gorilla has their own nest, except for infants and their mothers. These beds are made of grasses, leaves, and twigs. Young gorillas or females may make their nests in the trees.

He patrols ahead, always looking out for threats. He'll fight to protect his family.

The dominant silverback makes all the decisions about when his troop travels, when they eat, and when they rest. Other silverbacks in the group will sometimes trail behind the troop as they move to protect them from predators. Silverbacks have even been known to remove poachers' snares from the hands and feet of members of his troop.

Even at the cost of his own life.

The dominant silverback will fight a rival male, a predator, a poacher, or any other threat. His primary goal is the safety of his troop, even above his own safety.

When gorillas lose a member of the troop, they will touch, groom, poke, and lick the body.

Another silverback steps up. He will lead
the troop, teach, and protect.

When the dominant silverback passes or grows too old to maintain his place in the troop, another will rise to fill his spot as leader and protector.

He will sire his own young.

Females are mature at about ten years old. This is when many leave to find another troop. They may have offspring about every three to six years. Like humans, gorillas have a gestation period of nine months. The babies usually weigh about 4 or 5 pounds at birth and are dependent upon their mother for the first two to three years of their lives.

Tiny and fragile, this young male will grow.
He will build strength and learn gentleness.
He will follow his elders until, one day,
he too will lead.

The young gorilla becomes independent at about three years old. Before that, other gorillas hold, carry, groom, and play with the infant. Males reach maturity at about fifteen years old and may leave the group in order to find other females and possibly form their own troops.

"5TF: 5 Things You Didn't Know About Mountain Gorillas (Gorilla Beringei Beringei)!"
Dian Fossey Gorilla Fund. July 11, 2019. https://gorillafund.org/5tf-mountain-gorillas/

"Gorilla." World Wildlife Fund. Accessed October 20, 2020. https://www.worldwildlife.org/species/gorilla

"Gorillas Surviving in the Jungle Mountains | Gorillas in the Mountain Mist." *Real Wild*. February 3, 2018.
YouTube. https://www.youtube.com/watch?v=X8SjuJJowmM

"The Gorilla King," 3 July 2011. *Nature*. PBS. https://www.pbs.org/wnet/nature/the-gorilla-king-video-full-episode/5377/

"Home | Dian Fossey Gorilla Fund." 2021. Dian Fossey Gorilla Fund International, Inc. https://gorillafund.org/

"Mountain Gorilla." *National Geographic*. September 21, 2018.
https://www.nationalgeographic.com/animals/mammals/m/mountain-gorilla/

Tagg, Nikki. "Gorilla Guide: Where They Live, Diet, and Conservation" 2013. *Discover Wildlife*.
https://www.discoverwildlife.com/animal-facts/mammals/facts-about-gorillas/

"Titus—The Gorilla King." BBC. 2008 –2009. https://www.youtube.com/watch?v=4j5xWFS-zo4. https://www.bbc.co.uk/programmes/b00fm6v7

"Top 10 Facts about Mountain Gorillas." World Wildlife Fund. Accessed October 20, 2020.
https://www.wwf.org.uk/learn/fascinating-facts/gorillas

King, Barbara J. "Video: An Interspecies Flying Lesson." NPR. November 16, 2017.
https://www.npr.org/sections/13.7/2017/11/16/564319826/video-an-interspecies-flying-lesson

"Mountain Gorilla." African Wildlife Foundation. December 13, 2018. https://www.awf.org/wildlife-conservation/mountain-gorilla